AF079254

This book belongs to:

....

Using This Book

- Use the scenarios in this book as starting points for discussions with your child. Ask them to find the picture stickers and answer the questions.

- Use the star stickers to praise their successes, and to encourage good habits for school.

- Fill in the 'I will' tasks on the wipe-clean reward chart, and the star targets and rewards. Your child will enjoy joining in with this too, particularly in choosing the rewards. They will love the sense of responsibility, and the motivation of working towards the treats they've chosen.

- Rewards need not be big, but they should be meaningful to your child: an extra bedtime story, baking a cake, going to the swimming pool or the park, having a friend to play, a pocket money treat – something that they enjoy, and that you feel is appropriate for what they have achieved.

- Always keep a positive attitude and focus on their achievements. Never deny a reward that has been agreed and earned.

- Your child will soon appreciate that learning positive early habits will help to encourage them to grow to be responsible, thoughtful and successful.

ISBN 978-1-78270-064-7

Copyright © Award Publications Limited

All rights reserved. No part of this publication may be reproduced or utilised in any form or by any means electronic or mechanical, including photocopying, recording, or by any information storage and retrieval system now known or hereafter invented, without the prior written permission of the publisher.

Published by Award Publications Limited,
The Old Riding School, Welbeck,
Worksop, S80 3LR

/awardpublications @award.books
www.awardpublications.co.uk

24-1141 7

Printed in China

The Children's Book of
SUCCESS AT
SCHOOL

Sophie Giles

Illustrated by Kate Davies

AWARD PUBLICATIONS LIMITED

Terrible Timekeeping

Jane stayed up late last night watching television and forgot to set her alarm clock. This morning she overslept and has missed the bus, so Dad has to rush to take her to school. Jane will be in trouble for being late.

Why is Jane late for school?

Terrific Timekeeping

Jane now goes to bed earlier, and sets her alarm clock to wake her in plenty of time to catch the bus. She has even earned team points at school for her good timekeeping.

I arrive at school in plenty of time

Are you punctual?

Not Being Responsible

Josh forgot to give his parents the letter from the teacher about a school trip. So he has to stay in the classroom today and do school work while his classmates go on a day trip to the zoo.

Why can't Josh go to the zoo?

Being Responsible

Now Josh checks inside his school bag each night to make sure he remembers to pass on any letters that are sent home. Next week the class will go swimming after school – and Josh is going, too!

Are you responsible?

Poor Preparation

Anup is the star striker, but he can't play in the big football match today because he forgot to give his football kit to his dad to wash. His teammates will be very disappointed with him.

Why will the team be disappointed with Anup?

Being Prepared

Now Anup understands that his lack of preparation affects other people as well as himself. He is careful to think about what he needs for school each day. And of course he takes extra care of his football kit!

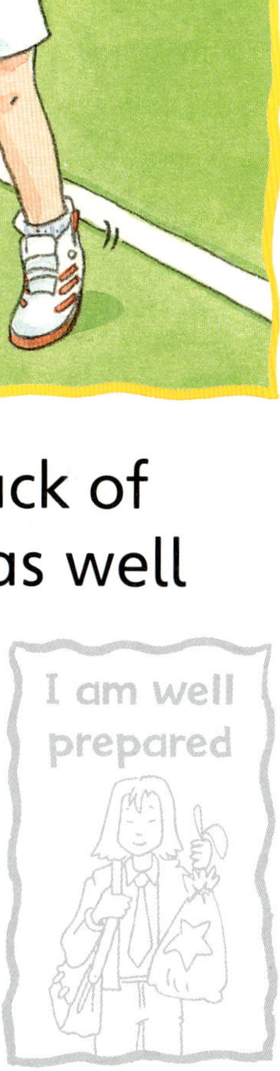

Are you well prepared?

Not Listening in Class

In the classroom the rule is to listen when the teacher is talking. But best friends Kabir and Penny keep chatting, so their teacher makes them sit at separate tables.

Why have Kabir and Penny been separated?

Listening in Class

Kabir and Penny have apologised to their teacher and now save their chatter for breaktime. Now that they listen properly in class, they are allowed to sit together again.

Do you listen properly in class?

I listen in class

Shouting Out

Kira is spoiling the lesson because she keeps shouting out the answers. Her classmates are unhappy because they want a chance to show they know the answer, too. The teacher tells Kira off.

How is Kira upsetting her classmates?

Hands Up

Now Kira puts up her hand and waits to be asked to answer questions. This means everyone has the chance to earn reward points for correct answers. Look at their reward chart – it is packed with stars!

Do you wait your turn in class?

I wait my turn to speak in class

Not Sharing

Jake was given a new basketball for his birthday, but he won't let anyone else play with it. When some of his classmates try to join his game, Jake picks up his ball and refuses to play with the other children.

What is selfish about Jake's behaviour?

Playing Together

When one of Jake's classmates rides her new scooter to school and lets everyone have a go, Jake feels bad. He apologises for not sharing, and at lunchtime the whole class enjoys a game of basketball with Jake's ball.
Do you share?

I make sure I always share

Copying Others

Artie has copied the work of his best friend, Ben, in a spelling test because he didn't bother to learn the spellings. But when they are awarded a prize for coming joint first, Artie feels guilty and lets Ben have the prize.

Why does Artie feel guilty?

Doing Your Own Work

Artie makes sure he prepares for class tests now, and he and Ben practise their spellings together after school. Artie hasn't come top of the class again yet, but he's proud of the stars that he has earned.

I do my own work

Do you do your own work?

Bullies

Freya's friend Amelia is being teased by some girls from another class. Freya is too scared to say anything to the girls, so she doesn't try to help, even though Amelia is upset and crying.

Why does Freya feel bad?

Telling a Teacher

The next day, the bullies tease Amelia again. Freya tells a teacher what they have been saying. He stops the other girls from teasing Amelia, and is pleased with Freya for helping her friend. **Would you tell a teacher about bullies?**

Not Doing Your Homework

Last week, Kim's class were asked to write a short story for their homework, but Kim thought it was silly and didn't do it. When a famous author came in to school to read the children's stories and pick a winner, Kim could not join in.
Why was Kim left out?

Doing Your Homework

Kim has learnt the importance of homework. It helps you to learn more and can show teachers if you are understanding the work – it can even be preparation for something fun! Kim always does her homework now!
Do you do your homework?

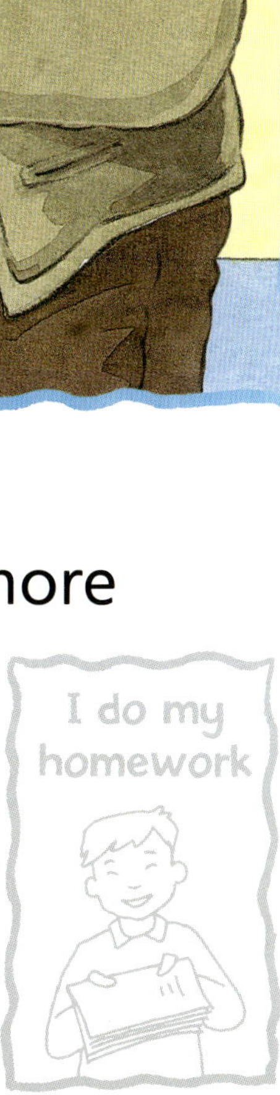

Excluding Others

Rafal is very nervous. He is new in school and doesn't know anyone. When the bell rings for morning playtime the other children all play together, but no one asks Rafal to join in. He feels very lonely.

Why is Rafal nervous?

Making Friends

James sees Rafal standing alone in the playground and goes over to say hello. Rafal likes the same music as James and they chat for the whole break. Back in class, James asks Rafal to sit next to him.

Are you friendly to others?

I am friendly

Being Bossy

Martha's class are working in groups to make a Roman fort. But Martha doesn't listen to the other children's ideas; she keeps telling them what she wants. Now no one wants to work with her.

Why does no one want Martha in their group?

Working Together

Martha has learned that it is better when people listen to one another and share ideas and the work that needs to be done. She understands that they can achieve more if they work together, and each take turns to lead the group.
Do you work well in a group?

Being Inconsiderate

Some children have left their lunch table in a mess. There are dirty plates and spilt drinks on the table. The lunchtime supervisor calls the children back to tidy the table so that others can sit there to eat their lunch.

Why is the supervisor cross?

Thinking of Others

The children clear away their plates after they have finished and wipe up any mess. They leave the table just as they found it – clean and tidy, ready for other children to sit down to eat.

I am considerate

Do you think of others?

Not Helping

Mr Castle is carrying a big pile of books and can't open the door. Jack and Mia say hello to him but then carry on with their game. Mr Castle tries to open the door, but he drops all of the books.

How could Jack and Mia have helped Mr Castle?

Being Helpful

Jack and Mia see Mr Castle struggling to open the door and they rush to help him before he drops the books he is carrying. They walk with him to the library and open the doors for him on the way.

Are you helpful at school?

Make an Origami Snapdragon

Making and playing with origami snapdragons (also known as salt cellars or fortune tellers) is a fun activity to share with your school-friends. You can use them to tell fortunes, set challenges or quizzes for your friends, or to revise for tests! But remember to only play during breaks, not in class.

You will need:

✔ an A4 piece of paper
✔ colour pencils or felt-tip pens

Preparing Your Paper

1. Fold in the bottom right corner of the paper.

2. Then fold in the bottom left corner. Trim off the rectangle, and recycle.

Cut off this part

3. Open out the remaining paper to reveal a square.

Folding Your Paper

1. Fold in each of the four corners to the middle.

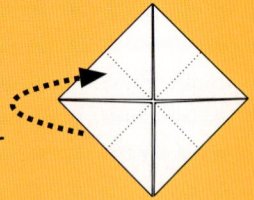

2. Then turn the paper over and lay it flat.

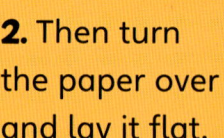

3. Now fold in each corner again, and turn the whole snapdragon over.

4. With the side with the four square flaps face up, fold the paper in half.

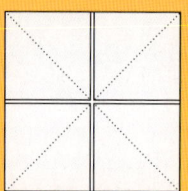 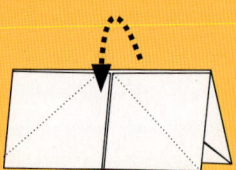

5. Gently push your thumbs and index fingers into the four flaps and open out to form the snapdragon. Finally, add your own design and questions.

How to Play

To move the snapdragon, first pinch your thumbs and index fingers together and gently pull outwards. Then bring your thumbs and fingers into the middle again, before pushing your index fingers and thumbs apart. As it opens and closes the eight options inside are revealed.

"Tell a Fortune" or Challenge Your Friends

1. Holding the snapdragon closed, ask a friend to choose one of the four outer squares.

2. Then open and close the snapdragon as you count out the number, or the letters of the word chosen. For example, for the word 'blue' open and close the snapdragon four times.

3. Ask your friend to pick one of the inner sections and again shuffle the snapdragon once for every letter of the word, or count out the numbers.

4. Now ask your friend to choose another one of the inner flaps. Fold out the flap to reveal their "fortune" or to set a challenge!

Quiz Time

Ask a friend to choose a subject from the four outer squares. Then open the snapdragon and ask them one of the questions for that subject. Lift the flap to see if they are right!

Get Revising!

Pick a sum on an outer square. Then move the snapdragon the number of times that is answer, and do one of the next sums that are revealed. Check the answer under the flap.

Snapdragon Designs

Here are some ideas for different types of snapdragon, but you can have lots of fun creating your own colourful designs to share with your friends.

What Will I Be?

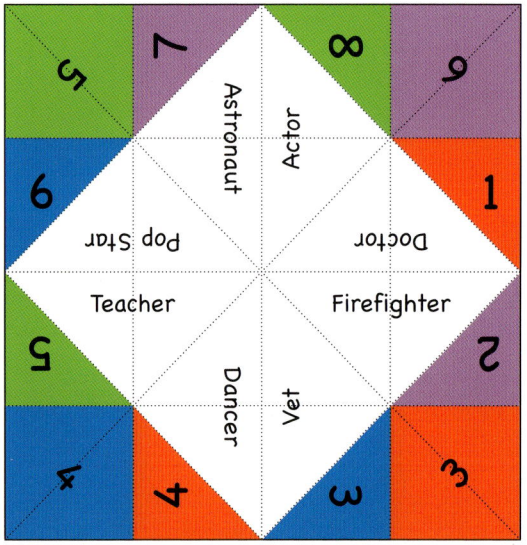

Champion Challenge!

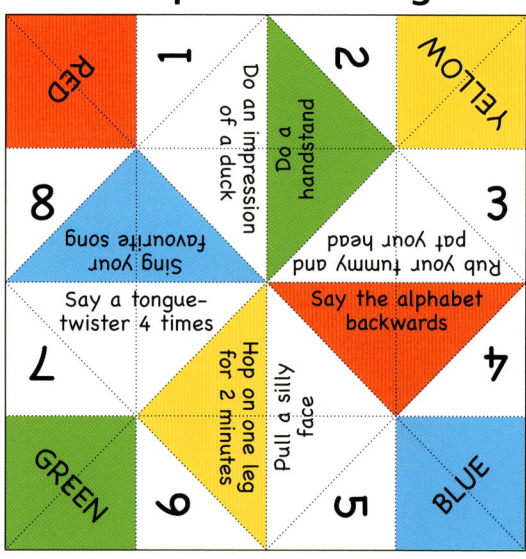

Quick Quiz

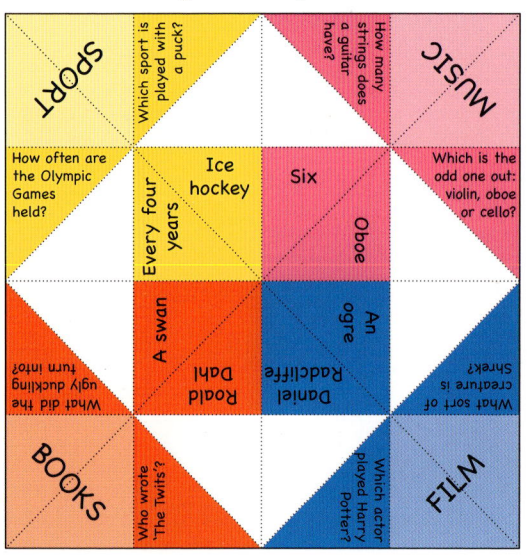

Times Tables Tester

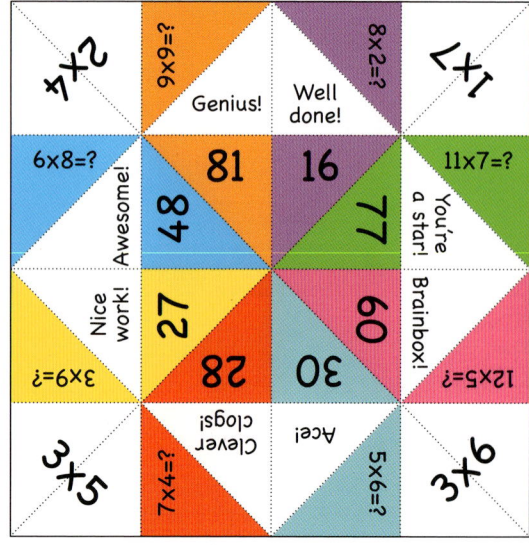

Encourage your child to use the picture stickers and answer the questions in the book.

 I make sure I always share

 I arrive at school in plenty of time

 I do my homework

I am responsible with letters sent home

I listen in class

I do my own work

I am considerate

 I am well prepared

I am friendly

I am helpful at school

 I work well in a group

I help to stop bullying

I wait my turn to speak in class